Miss Myrtle Frag
the Grammar Nag

LaWanda Bailey

Illustrated by Brian Strassburg

Absey & Company
Spring, Texas

ISBN 1-888842-19-9
Designed by Edward E. Wilson

Dedication

For my parents, Carl and Nadine Akin, who
are models of unconditional love

Acknowledgments

While writing this book, I repeated the cycle of collaboration followed by hours of solitary creation. I am fortunate to have had access to a great many innovative thinkers. Thanks, first of all, to Richard, my husband, for his intelligent wit and unwavering support. To Eileen Standridge, who sits on the board of directors for my life, I owe gratitude for splendid mentorship. Wanda Bellar, Karen Ferrell, and Kathy Knowles were always there to give honest critiques. Teachers in writing institutes and students in classrooms helped me know what would and would not work.

Scores of friends have pushed me to publish over the years, and I thank all of them, but especially these: Polly and Deane Haerer, Dr. Jimmy McLeod, Gloria North, Johnnie Steele, and Pat Dickinson.

My family encouraged me and did without me nights and weekends while I wrote after work. I look forward to long hours with them: Tony and Kristy, Shanna and Martin, Austin and Brittany, Mom and Dad, Sandy and Bobby, Dot and George, Jon and Melanie, Steve, James Carl, Tony and Danielle, Andrew, Brandon, Sarah, and Hilda.

I thank Dr. Joyce Armstrong Carroll and Edward E. Wilson for the opportunity to write and for the incredible training that they have made available to thousands through the New Jersey Writing Project in Texas. Trey Hall, my editor, has given me great freedom, and I appreciate his wise counsel.

And finally, my thanks go to my Northwest ISD family and to the memory of Miss Jane Etheridge, my relentless high school English teacher, for sharing her love of grammar with me.

Introduction

Miss Frog had knocked on the door of my imagination for several weeks. Then one morning, she walked right in and made herself at home. I had been searching for a way to present grammar rules in a non-threatening manner during a summer workshop, and *Miss Frog* began to take on a life of her own.

The spoken word *grammar* can clear a room in fifteen seconds, for its very name often implies rigor, agony, sweaty palms, and red marks on papers. To others, grammar is ethereal, worthy of devotion. In truth, grammar is simply the study of the language that we already know how to speak. True, some are more fluent than others, but most use language amazingly well, and did so long before they entered school. To make a comparison, a person doesn't have to know how a car engine works to drive the car; but those who do know generally get maximum benefit from their vehicles. They understand maintenance and don't stand wringing their hands when they find themselves on the roadside during traffic. Likewise, people communicate with meaning and can function quite nicely in the world without studying their language. However, those who understand how language works find that they increase their options in a world that values correct speech and writing, especially during this computer age when more people than ever are communicating.

In my search to make grammar more inviting , I turned to well-known experts. I am a teacher of writing; not necessarily a guru of grammar. However, for decades I have enjoyed the study of language and have edited extensively throughout my professional life. I also wrote and edited full-time for an independent educational publisher. Then I immersed myself for a year in the study of noted authorities in the field, and I leaned heavily on their research throughout the writing of this book. Their collective views are mirrored throughout this work, and I admire them greatly. You will find them listed, along with some other interesting authors, on the reference page at the end of the book.

The challenge remained: how to make students (or anyone) remember grammar rules. My answer came as I reflected on chance meetings with former students. I had been a classroom teacher for twenty-one years, long enough for my former middle school students to become college graduates, mothers, teachers, and such. Almost without fail, former students greet me with the memory of a story I told in class. One young man said that he could still remember the location of countries from the stories I made up in social studies. Others remember the spelling rule chanted by cheerleaders in a story. Just this fall, a former student began teaching in our district, and the first thing she mentioned to me was a story I had told about a talking dog. Today I know about brain research and the power of story, but back then I just knew that I had found something that worked.

I decided to bring story and grammar together in the summer workshop, and *Miss Frog* evolved as my vehicle. She is a blend of teachers we have known. Part of her is the stereotypical English teacher from another time, with a ruler in one hand, a red pen in the other, and a withering scowl ready for grammar offenders. But she is reformed. She has entered the Information Age aware of what research has to say about learning. She reluctantly acknowledges that language changes over time. You will find her at odds with herself throughout the book, but her heart is always in the right place.

When I teach from this book, I choose the parts I need for given grade levels or class personalities. Clearly, most of the rules addressed are more intermediate and secondary in nature. With younger students, I don't share *Miss Frog's* letter exchange. I tell the story in their vernacular or use some of its characters to enforce a rule. I also use a story as the springboard for them to create their own stories about the rules they are studying that year. More mature students enjoy the letters. Some classes like to have the stories read;

others prefer a telling. Almost all benefit from sketches, no matter how simple, for added impact. In line with research, I then send students into literature and their own writing to find examples of the grammar rule.

Opinions vary on the definition of grammar. Lines are drawn with mechanics on this side, usage on that side; parts of speech here, syntax there. Since the purpose of this book is to have fun with rules while helping people gain better understanding and control of written and spoken language, I chose to address grammar globally.

I never planned to write this book; I was simply looking for a way to have fun with grammar rules. I did nothing more than good teachers everywhere do day after day. My goal is that story will give people memory hooks onto which they can hang the deeper understandings that occur from further study. Maybe a former student will come to you someday and remind you of one of these ridiculous stories. Don't forget that you can always blame *Miss Myrtle Frog*.

11

Dear Miss Myrtle Frag,

　　You have to help me! All week long, my students focused on punctuating quoted material within their original stories. I thought they had it. Now I'm sitting at home grading their papers, my red pen shaking uncontrollably. Punctuation marks are scattered with reckless abandon throughout their compositions. Please put me out of my misery!

2|

Sincerely,
Traumatized Teacher

Dear Teacher,

    First of all, my dear, Miss Frag urges you to pry the red pen out of your hand and drop it into the nearest wastebasket. You may experience a rigor or two (as did Miss Frag some years ago), but you and your students will benefit. Now take a few deep breaths, tuck the papers back into your canvas tote bag, and read this little story:

Don't Fence Me In or Out

Once upon a time, the Quotation family built a picket fence. It looked like this " " " " " " all around their house. Because they were so tiny, little Tommy Commy (,) and his sister Dot (.) were forbidden to wander outside the fence. On the other hand, their older siblings S.C. (; Semicolon) and D.D. (: Double Dot) were ordered to stay outside the fence so as not to annoy the younger children. As leaders of the family, Mother (?) and Father (!) would move either inside or outside the fence as they were needed.

Now, would you believe that Tommy Commy (,) and Dot (.) tried to slip under the fence on certain occasions? S.C. (;) and D.D. (:) whined every day, wanting to step inside the pickets. Poor Mother and Father, worn out from running back and forth, longed to stay in the same place all of the time. But the Quotation family did not get their wishes granted, even though they begged shamelessly. Readers and writers everywhere demanded that they follow the rules. So to this day, they stay where they belong.

During your next class, return the students' papers, tell them the story, and let them correct their own errors! You might want to know that the only times you will see exceptions to these rules are in internal documentation of sources and in some British literature. Now you can drink a glass of warm milk and climb into |5 bed. Miss Frag hopes that she has calmed you. Goodnight, dear teacher.

Yours truly,
Miss Myrtle Frag

The Rules

Always place periods and commas inside quotation marks. (Exceptions: MLA in-text citations and some British literature). Put colons and semicolons outside quotation marks. Place question marks and exclamation points inside unless they apply to the entire sentence.

6| **Examples:**

"I am going to the water park," explained Rosa.

I like these words from "Ocean Sounds": *splash, whitetop, sandsteps.*

Joseph sang "My Buddy"; his friend sang "Jake Was a Good Dog."

"The house is on fire!" shouted Maya. "Are you coming?"

I love to hear Chris read "Rainbows"! Do you like it better than "Five Miles Away"?

DEAR MISS FRAG,

WHAT IS A CONTRAPTION? MY LANGUAGE ARTS TEACHER SAID THAT WE ARE GOING TO LEARN TO MAKE THEM. DAD SAYS HE CANNOT UNDERSTAND WHY WE WOULD BE MAKING CONTRAPTIONS IN AN ENGLISH CLASS. THANK YOU.

CONFUSED

Dear Confused,

   Miss Frag thinks that you misunderstood your teacher. He probably said that you were going to learn to make contractions. Contractions are shortened forms of words or phrases. For example, **THEY** and **WILL** become **THEY'LL**. You have given Miss Frag a lovely idea for a story, however. See if this helps you:

The Contraction Contraption

Words take vacations, too. If you don't believe me, how do you explain all of the times you've heard people say, "I can't think of the right word" or "I forgot what I was going to say"? At that exact moment, the missing words are having the times of their lives at an amusement park called Wordyworld!

On Pal Day, word pairs could get into the park half-price. As they passed through the ticket gate, Loquacia, the park manager, handed out coupons for a free ride on the new Contraction Contraption. The words scattered among stage shows, food booths, and rides, but within half an hour, most of them stood in a long line at the Contraction Contraption. As the words waited, they read the instructions that were hanging on the fence:

Must ride this ride in pairs
Not just any pairs, but words that can be shortened into a single word (contraction)
No bad words allowed

I and **am** were the first in line. They laughed nervously as they stepped onto the Contraction Contraption. The ride was made of metal and foam, nuts and bolts, rubber and tubes; it looked scary. With a jerk, the conveyor belt pulled **I** and **am** out of sight. Within ten seconds, the giant mechanical device whirled, rocked, rattled and roared. SHABOOM! The ride spit the letter **a** out of a tube on top. The **a** shot almost out of sight. The words waiting in line applauded as it finally descended into a storage net above the ride.

In an instant, the other two letters swooshed down a slide and landed side by side like this: **I m**. Directly above them, a giant container tipped over and dropped an apostrophe right where the missing a had once stood. Then they looked like this: **I'm.**

Laughing with delight, the contraction dropped through a trap door that rolled it out at the end of the ride. Next, **has** and **not** rode the Contraction Contraption, followed by **you** and **have** and the other word pairs.

The words discovered that they could go through the ride backwards and return to the way they used to be. They were having so much fun making and undoing contractions that **we've, let's, I'd,** and **it's** missed the bus home. Just as they were about to panic, the park's wordwatcher drove up in a shiny new voCAB and offered to take them home. "Good thing you are in your contracted forms, or you wouldn't all fit," he laughed.

They arrived home shortly after their friends on the bus got there, and people everywhere started saying, "Now I remember what I was going to say!" Wouldn't they be surprised if they knew that their words had just returned from Wordyworld?

Miss Frag warns you about two things: Be certain that you take out the right letters, and be careful to place the apostrophe in the exact spot where the missing letters stood. Wise writers check their papers for misused apostrophes.

Miss Myrtle Frag

The Rules

A contraction is a word or phrase that has been shortened. When letters are left out to make the word or phrase shorter, an apostrophe is used to replace the missing letters.

Examples:

cannot	can't
are not	aren't
he is	he's
could not	couldn't
of the clock	o'clock
it is	it's

Tip: It's easy to confuse contractions with possessives (its, it's) and with words that sound alike (their, they're).

|4|

Independent

SUBORDINATE and **CLAUSES**

15

Dear Miss F,

Hey, I've got this problem here, Baby! My teacher, she said that I ain't never gonna pass her class. Because I can't learn about independent and subordinate clauses. Like I care about grammar. Ha! But I do care about getting my driver's license and my old man says that ain't gonna happen if I don't pass. So anyway, my teacher told me to write you. If you can help get me behind the wheel. I'll wave to you when we pass each other on the freeway. V-room, Baby!

Spike

Dear Spike,

　You have rendered Miss Frag speechless. She is answering this letter with an ice pack pressed to her forehead. First, let Miss Frag assure you that any help she gives you is not prompted by a desire to see you behind the wheel. To the contrary, she thinks that you would benefit from several years of lock-up in a grammar jail until the connecting pathways in your brain are fully developed. Perhaps this little story will help you grow a dendrite or two, young man:

The Real Santa CLAUSe

A department store Santa, no longer content being a subordinate CLAUSe, decided that he wanted to be the real Santa CLAUSe. Why should his own world be filled with screaming children and flashing cameras while the real Santa played with computer games and traveled around the world? The subordinate CLAUSe, having had enough of whistling and shouting and calling kids by name, decided to assess the situation. What did the independent CLAUSe have that he didn't have? He made a list and checked it twice:

Independent CLAUSe's Qualities	Subordinate CLAUSe's Qualities
has a subject	has a subject
has a predicate	has a predicate
sometimes has a complement	sometimes has a complement
	sometimes does the work of a noun
	sometimes does the work of an adjective
	sometimes does the work of an adverb

"Ho! Ho! Ho!" the subordinate CLAUSe exclaimed, reeling with excitement. He had all of the independent CLAUSe's qualities and more! Within minutes, he called Santa to come for an urgent meeting, all the while making plans to lock him away in the mall for Christmas Eve.

Then he went straight to his work, stuffing each of his qualities into a separate bundle. The subordinate CLAUSe flung the bags on his back, laughed, and stood to leave. But, alas, something unforeseen happened. Just as he stood, the noun, adjective, and adverb bundles pulled him off balance. Crash! He fell backwards into the decorated tree. After struggling to his feet, he shifted the bundles across his forearm and sprawled forward directly into the fireplace.

All covered with ashes and soot, he kept trying to stand. But the noun, adjective, and adverb bags kept toppling him over. After fifteen tries, he sat on the floor and wept, his dreams for independence gone.

And then in a twinkling, the independent CLAUSe appeared, carrying his subject, predicate, and sometimes-complement bundles. He lifted the subordinate CLAUSe to his feet. They stood side by side, and the weaker CLAUSe found that he no longer toppled.

They could have passed for twins. The only apparent difference was that the subordinate CLAUSe held more bundles. If only he had known his grammar rules, he could have found an easy solution to his problem. But he greedily clutched the extra bags, still thinking they made him stronger. To this day, the subordinate CLAUSe can be found in compositions, leaning against the independent CLAUSe in order to stand.

Miss Frag, normally a person of great compassion, regrets the negative nature of her answer. However, she is unaccustomed to the lack of respect displayed in your letter, Spike. To her loyal readers, Miss Frag issues a warning to be ever alert for a young, reckless driver speeding along and screaming "V-room, Baby!"

Miss Myrtle Frag

20|

The Rules

An independent clause can stand alone. Sometimes it stands all by itself. At other times, it is part of a larger sentence, but it could stand alone if removed from that sentence. It has a subject and a predicate, and sometimes it has a complement. |21

A subordinate clause looks a lot like an independent clause (sentence). It has a subject and a predicate, and sometimes it has a complement. However, because it does the work of a noun, an adjective, or an adverb in a sentence, it cannot stand alone if removed from the sentence.

Examples independent and subordinate clauses:

Ricardo walked toward the pond.
 (independent clause)

Ricardo walked toward the pond, and **his young cousin climbed a tree.**
(two independent clauses)

While Ricardo walked toward the pond, his young cousin climbed a tree.
(**subordinate clause doing the work of an adverb,** independent clause)

The young cousin **who followed Ricardo** climbed a tree.
(subordinate clause doing the work of an adjective)

Whoever finds Ricardo will find his young cousin.
(subordinate clause doing the work of a noun)

Dear Miss Frag,

What's a comma splice? I have to know right now so I can correct my paper. I would ask my teacher, but she's crying pretty hard and mumbling, "I can't stand to see one more comma splice!" I called 911 first, they didn't know. Do you?

24|

frantic

Dear Frantic,

You must act quickly. Find a place in your paper where you have two independent clauses (sentences) stuck together with a comma. That is known as comma splice. In Miss Frag's day, it was called a comma fault. One way to repair this atrocity of the writing world is to change the comma to a semicolon. Now, slowly pass the corrected paper in front of your teacher. This should bring her around. |25

Now that the emergency is over, borrow one of your teacher's tissues and prepare to weep. Miss Frag will share a sad little tale with you:

It Was the Comma's Fault

A suspension bridge swayed securely across a gorge which separated Clauseville from Clausetown.

26

Two parts of the bridge (,) and (and), tired of just hanging around day after boring day, decided to go on a series of adventures. They asked their friend (;) to take their place in the bridge, and off they went.

Most of the bridge parts never noticed the difference. Even in the brisk wind, the bridge swayed normally. Then, as luck would have it, (;) had to leave in an instant due to a family emergency. (Colon problems ran in her family.) As she rushed away, she called back for her friend (.) to stand in her place on the bridge.

Luckily, (.) possessed all of the strength he needed to hold the two clauses together. The citizens who traveled over the bridge, however, complained that their trip was choppier with two sentences to cross. Unfortunately, (.) was spoiled due to his popularity, and he vowed to teach the grumbling travelers a lesson. Yes, he would show them! Quietly, he planned an ending (his specialty).

Without warning, (.) did a splashy cannonball into the river below. From the cliff (,) watched in horror. She was known for her quickness, and just as the bridge began to creak, she jumped into the vacated spot.

The citizens applauded her. But their cheers turned to screams as the bridge began to wobble and groan. Slowly at first, and then violently, words collided, and the bridge fell shattered into the river below. She might have been fast, but (,) was not strong enough to hold the two clauses together.

Residents of Clauseville and Clausetown, now forever separated, gathered above the gorge and shouted, "It was the comma's fault!" But we know that (.) caused the unhappy ending.

Miss Frag asks that you help save the commas. They are on her endangered list due to their overuse. A trend is developing to use the comma splice in informal pieces when the clauses are brief and closely connected in meaning. Miss Frag suspects that in time this will become acceptable. She just hopes that she has gone on to her well-deserved reward in the hereafter before that happens. Poor little commas were not created to handle industrial-strength jobs. Oh, my! This emergency work has tired Miss Frag. She must recline before she faints.

Miss M. Frag

The Rule

Comma splices are independent clauses that have not been joined correctly. When two independent clauses appear in one sentence, a comma is too weak to connect them. Join them in one of these ways:

1. Comma with a coordinating conjunction (and, but, or, for, nor, yet)
2. Semicolon (or sometimes a dash or a colon)
3. Make two sentences

Examples:

Derek got a drum set for his birthday, **and** his neighbors sold their house the next month.

Derek got a drum set for his birthday**;** his neighbors sold their house the next month.

Derek got a drum set for his birthday. His neighbors sold their house the next month.

DEAR MISS FRAG,

MY ENGLISH TEACHER SAYS I NEED TO EDIT MY PAPERS. BECAUSE I USE TOO MANY FRAGMENTS. I TRY TO EDIT. READING MY PAPERS CAREFULLY. WHEN I DO FIND A FRAGMENT. I DON'T KNOW HOW TO FIX IT. CAN YOU HELP ME?

BITSY. FROM SCRAP GAP

32|

Dear Bitsy,

Fragments are imposters! They try in every way possible to look like real sentences, and they fool many writers. You will be able to find fragments more easily if you understand independent and subordinate clauses (see story about clauses). Just remember that a group of words must be able to stand alone to be a sentence. Miss Frag composed this little story just for you:

Snobby Sentence Ball

The Society of Snobby Sentences gathered for the annual Snobby Sentence Ball. Each sentence arrived standing alone, making sense, and dressed exquisitely in subjects and verbs.

A few slipped in as simple sentences; others who had shopped the two-for-one sales attended as compound sentences. The complex sentences, as always, entered with their subordinate clauses draped lavishly over their shoulders. When the arrogant compound-complex sentences swaggered in, the other sentences rolled their i's in disgust.

Comments like these floated throughout the room as the sentences bragged and gossiped:

"Don't we look fabulous?" the interrogative sentences asked as they whirled around the dance floor.

"What a pitiful simple subject you wore!" an exclamatory sentence shouted to a short, choppy sentence across the room.

"Go back home and revise yourself," a brash imperative sentence sneered as an awkward sentence stumbled through the door.

As a new member strutted by, the declarative sentences snipped, "Her verb looks irregular to us."

They were all terribly conceited. However, on one point they agreed: they all loathed fragments! The snobs hated how they pretended to be sentences. Sometimes the frags wore a subject or predicate (or both!), but they had to cling to other groups of words for steadiness. Last year, the low-down frags had crashed their dance, but this year would be different. With great care, the snobs had concealed two fragment detectors on the ceiling. Frag Snagger One would scan for subjects and verbs while Frag Snagger Two looked for subordinating words such as **because** and **if**.

As the sentences glided across the dance floor, Frag Snagger Two detected a fragment and clanged loudly. Just as the device started to shine a light on **Because we're sneakier than you are**, the snagged frag quickly began to dance with a nearby sentence. Together, they looked like this: **You can't catch us because we're sneakier than you are**. To the snobby sentences' horror, the fragment no longer existed.

And so it went all night. Whenever a fragment was identified, it either attached itself to a nearby sentence or made itself into a sentence by adding the needed words. Frag Snagger One located **Especially the party crashers**. The fragment quickly created some words on its own until it was a sentence: **Everyone enjoyed the ball, especially the party crashers.**

Members of the Society of Snobby Sentences, embarrassed at being outwitted by the lowly fragments, poured out of the exit doors, losing all of their dignity. Some tripped and split their infinitives; others left with their verbs tense. A few tumbled and became inverted; many limped home with misplaced modifiers and dangling participles. One sentence mumbled, "Nothing can mess up a good party like fragments!" (They do that to good writing, too.)

Miss Frag hopes that you can edit more easily now. Just be aware that fragments are deceptive. Sometimes they are used on purpose for effect. However, most of the time, they are just try-ing to crash your writing like they crashed the sentences' party. Miss Frag urges you to look at your own letter again. Several frags are hiding within.

Miss Myrtle Frag

The Rule

A fragment is a word group that might look like a sentence, but it cannot stand alone. These are some of the disguises that a fragment might wear:

- It might have a subject.
- It might have a predicate.
- It might have a subject and predicate, but also a subordinating word.
- It might have neither a subject nor a predicate.

Examples:

I saw two of my favorite teachers. **Mrs. Ingram and my football coach.**

(The bolded word group is a **fragment**. *Mrs. Ingram* and *coach* look like subjects, but there is no predicate in their word group.)

Two (of many) ways to fix it:

I saw two of my favorite teachers: Mrs. Ingram and my football coach.

I saw two of my favorite teachers. Mrs. Ingram and my football coach came to the awards banquet.

Mr. Escamilla smiled happily. **When his son won the award**.

(The bolded word group is a **fragment**. *Son* looks like a sentence subject, and *won* looks like the predicate. *When* is a subordinating word that makes the word group unable to stand alone.)

Two (of many) ways to fix it:

Mr. Escamilla smiled happily when his son won the award.

Mr. Escamilla smiled happily. When his son won the award, he was a very proud father.

My cat sleeps in the same place each night. **Under my bed**.

(The bolded word group is a **fragment**. It has neither a subject nor a predicate.)

Two (of many) ways to fix it:

My cat sleeps in the same place each night--under my bed.

My cat sleeps in the same place each night. She feels safe under my bed.

Tip: Writers may choose to use a fragment for emphasis, in an exclamation, in answer to a question, or to make a transition. When used for a purpose, fragments are acceptable.

Colons

Dear Miss Myrtle Frag, the Grammar Nag:

As you can tell from my precise salutation, I am quite proper. I spend most of my time writing business letters for two reasons: I love to use the colon, and I haven't room in my absolutely perfect mind for enough warmth to write a friendly letter. I am weary of reading letter replies from those who seem to be unschooled in the uses of colons. I fear that most of my correspondents come from the shallow end of the gene pool, if I may speak metaphorically. I write to you, Miss Frag, in hopes that you can clarify colon rules for the profoundly average people with whom we must share the world.

Sincerely,
Beatrice Betterthaneveryone

40|

Dear Ms. Betterthaneveryone:

Miss Frag understands you completely, for she once viewed the world from her grammar throne, if she may speak metaphorically. Miss Frag hastens to mention that she is glad that she abdicated before your rise to power. She has the distinct feeling that you would have taken the monarchy by force. While [41] it is true that some have better language control than others, many have gifts that you don't have. A pleasing personality leaps to mind as an example. Please consider sharing this story about colon uses rather than browbeating "the profoundly average" with your grammar stick.

Colonel Colon: Announcer

Colonel Colon was a proud member of the military. He was proud of his rank, proud of his well-trained troops, and proud that his last name appeared in his title. But most of all, he loved his job: announcing things.

Colonel Colon's prized possession was a specially made double trumpet. The bells of the double trumpet looked like this (:), and the colonel delighted in blowing it dozens of times a day as he made announcements. Unfortunately, he had skipped too many band classes in high school. When he blasted the trumpet, it sounded like *Tah dahdah Ta-a-a-h*, with the last note annoyingly off-key. His troops spent a lot of time with their hands over their ears.

One evening, he assembled the troops for his favorite drill. He ordered them to form independent clauses that would direct attention to the words that followed those clauses. Of course, Colonel Colon stood nearby, ready to jump in after the independent clauses. (Little did he know that his frustrated troops had held a meeting the night before and created a plan to go AWOL.). As he bellowed his commands, the troops formed the sentences they had planned:

Formation #1 (A list):

Please order the following: (tah dahdah Ta-a-a-h)

four hundred earplugs, headache medicine, and a smaller trumpet.

42

Formation #2 (A quotation):
Consider the words of a famous horn player: (tah dahdah Ta-a-a-h) "The first quality that is needed in a musician is talent."

Formation #3 (An appositive):
We have one dream: (tah dahdah Ta-a-a-h) a day with no announcements.

Formation #4 (Between two independent clauses when the last one explains the first):
Your troops are like range cattle: (tah dahdah Ta-a-a-h) They stampede when they hear a frightening noise.

With that, the troops broke into a mad run, their hands clasped over their ears. Colonel Colon looked everywhere for his missing soldiers. He dashed to the end of the salutation in a business letter; then he stood in a bibliography (between the city and publisher). He braced himself between a title and subtitle before standing between biblical chapters and verses. Then he jumped back and forth between the hour and minutes and the numbers in ratios.

Unable to cope with the loss of his troops, he left his military division. Now he blasts his double trumpet in writers' ears all over the country. Use a colon occasionally; it will make Colonel Colon happy. But don't overdo it. A reader can only take so many sour notes.

Miss Betterthaneveryone, while Miss Frag is often accused of being a grammar snob, she is not without warmth. As a matter of fact, she would rather spend an evening with the grammar-impaired than one moment in your company. Miss Frag abandons her legendary etiquette with this outburst: (tah dahdah Ta-a-a-h) Get a life!

M. Frag

The Rules

One of the most important jobs of the colon is to direct attention to the words that follow it. These words might be in the form of a list, a quotation, an appositive, or an explanation. When announcing, the colon always comes after a complete independent clause.

A colon is also used after the salutation of a business letter and to separate the following:

hours from minutes   (8:34)
numbers in a ratio   (4:1)
title from subtitle   (*Life Underground: An Ant's View of the World*)
city from publisher in a bibliography   (Ft. Worth: Knowles, 1999)
verse from chapter in the Bible   (John 3:16)

Examples:

(List)
While you're at the store, get the following: toothpaste, dog food, milk, eggs, and bread.

(Quotation)
Remember what Coach Martin said: "Never give up. Never, never, never give up."

(Appositive)
My grandmother has two great talents: cooking and golfing.

46

(Explanation)
LaTonya is like a butterfly: She flutters from friend to friend all day.

Tip: If an independent clause follows the colon, you may begin it with a capital or lowercase letter.

DEAR MISS MYRTLE FRAG,

I'M A FOOTBALL COACH WITH A DEGREE IN ENGLISH. MY NEWEST
THERAPIST THINKS THAT I AM IRRATIONAL OVER A PARTICULAR USAGE ERROR,
SO YOU ARE MY LAST RESORT. I'M THROWING THE YELLOW FLAG ON THE
USE OF I AS AN OBJECTIVE CASE PRONOUN. DURING THE SUMMER, I
WATCH THE 24-HOUR SPORTS CHANNEL SIXTEEN HOURS A DAY. TONIGHT'S
SPORTSCASTER, DASH RIPSNAP, PANCAKED ME WITH THIS SENTENCE: "WE
CAN ONLY HOPE THAT THIS NEVER HAPPENS TO YOU AND I." THAT THIS
NEVER HAPPENS TO you? THAT THIS NEVER HAPPENS TO I? HELP ME, MISS
MYRTLE. MY SANITY IS IN THE FOURTH QUARTER, AND I'M OUT OF TIME
OUTS. YOU DON'T THINK I'M CRAZY, DO YOU?

COACH PERCY SNODGRASS

Dear Coach,

Crazy? Never! You sound like the breath of sanity to Miss Frag. Whether she overhears tattooed, pierced teenagers in the mall or listens to formal lectures in great halls, Miss Frag hears this as one of the most common usage errors in society.

She suspects that the widespread misuse of the objective case in compound subjects started the problem that troubles you. For decades, we have endured misusages like "Mark and me went to town." Teachers have correctly cautioned students to say "Mark and I went to town" instead. Now, millions of people think that anytime there is a compound subject OR object, **me** is always replaced with **I**.

Miss Frag has prepared a special football story for you. Call and read it to Mr. Ripsnap. Your therapist evidently needs to hear it, too. His flippant attitude about this error troubles Miss Frag.

The Quarterback Sneak

A football player for Grammar University made a name for himself during a championship game. His name was Ivan, but people called him **I** for short. Because **I** was the quarterback, it was his job to throw the ball and make the action start.

Instead of being thrilled to hold such a respected position on the team, **I** felt miserable! More than anything, **I** wanted to be a receiver. So strong was his desire to receive that he apparently lost his mind during the final play of his final game at Grammar U. The other team's quarterback threw a long pass. **I** leaped off the bench, received the ball, and scored the winning touchdown for the opponents. The Grammarians, crazy with rage, screamed, "IGNORAMUS!" His coach tackled him in the end zone and yelled, "**I**, you are a doer, not a receiver! Do you hear me, **I**? You can't be a receiver!" His friends no longer called him **I**, but Ignoramus instead (not that he had any friends left). He remained the SUBJECT of discussion for decades.

Coach Snodgrass, may Miss Frag urge you to flip your remote control to the public television station on occasion? Face the fact that you have a double identity and do all you can to nurture your whole brain. Now, if you will excuse Miss Frag, she must|5| phone her therapist. Your use of **pancake** as a verb has brought on one of her anxiety attacks.

M. Frag

The Rule

When a pronoun functions as a direct object, an indirect object, or the object of a preposition, it must be in the objective case (me, us, you, him/her/it, them).

52 | Examples:

Josh and I threw the Frisbees to Dad. (subject; doer)
(*Josh threw the Frisbees. I threw the Frisbees.*)

Dad threw the Frisbees to Josh and *me*. (object; receiver)
(*Dad threw the Frisbees to Josh. Dad threw the Frisbees to me.*)

Tip: Mentally divide compound subjects and objects as in the examples above. You'll get it right!

Their, There, and They're

Dear Miss Myrtle Frag,

My teacher thinks I'm perfect. Miss Weaver says that I make fewer mistakes than anyone she has ever taught. That's quite an honor because this is her 73rd year of teaching. However, I live in fear that she will discover my secret flaw. Whenever I have to use *there, their,* or *they're,* my brain just spins. I find myself writing awkward sentences to avoid using one of those words incorrectly. After all, I must maintain my image. Here's an example of what I wrote on my last paper:

> Mr. Kwan and Lee took Mr. Kwan's and Lee's broken bicycles to Samantha's Repair Shop. When they got to Samantha'sRepair Shop, they asked her how long it would take to fix Mr. Kwan's and Lee's bicycles. She said, "It will take two weeks." Mr. Kwan and Lee are going to miss Mr. Kwan's and Lee's bikes.

My writing is error-free, but I wonder if it needs more flow. Can you help me overcome my fear of these three little words? I look forward to your answer, but right now Miss Weaver is waiting for me to water her plastic flowers.

Princess

Dear Princess,

Leave it to Weaver to make Miss Frag look like a free spirit! Miss Frag asks you to treat your vintage teacher with deep respect, but the plastic flower duty may be a clue that all is not well.

Miss Frag's brain did a quick spin of its own as she read your writing sample. As you know, she is thought by some to be a grammar snob, but she will disprove that revolting lie with this statement: Error-free writing is not always good writing. You are correct to wonder if your writing needs more flow. It doesn't even trickle, my dear. Miss Frag is nothing if not sensitive, so she will leave it at that. The **there, their, they're** problem is one of the most common ones in writing. Perhaps this story will help you reach total perfection:

Triple Trouble: A Tale of Deceit

Triplets! They looked so much alike that they confused everyone at school. The triplets, being quite mischievous, enjoyed playing tricks on each other and everyone else. One of them started a food fight in the lunchroom, and his brother ended up in the principal's office.   Another walked up to his brother's coach and said, "If you didn't treat us like sissies at practice, we might win a game." His brother's next practice was a nightmare! Almost every day, the triplets switched classes. Yes, THEIR, THERE, and THEY'RE spent much of their time in the wrong places.

Finally, desperate to end the charade, the school counselor planned a parent-teacher meeting. "Please," she begged the parents, "tell us how we can tell them apart." The teachers prepared to take notes.

"Perhaps it will help," said their mother, "for you to know how we chose their names. THEIR is the oldest by one minute. As our firstborn, he became HEIR to his grandfather's many possessions. Every time you see him, he has something that he owns with him. We're not proud of it, but he's a possessive little fellow. Just think of his name like tHEIR and look for what he owns."

Their dad picked up the explanation. "THERE is our active triplet. Even in his crib, he would be HERE when we put him down, and tHERE when we picked him up. When he's playing ball, he's everywHERE, and it drives his coaches crazy. Since he's always HERE and tHERE, we're often asking, 'wHERE's THERE?' Just think of his name like tHERE to remember location."

"That leaves THEY'RE," their mom continued. "He is the only one with a middle name. We actually named him THEY ARE, but his brothers knocked the **A** right out of him in a playpen brawl. We put the crushed **A** on ice and rushed to an editor, but she was unable to restore the letter. However, she assured us that the collapsed **A** looked a lot like an apostrophe, and that if we inserted it, our son's name would mean exactly the same thing. So just remember to think THEY^{A}RE when you see THEY'RE."

The secret was out! The next day, teachers told all of the triplets' classmates how to tell them apart. Unable to stand the boredom of following the rules, the threesome decided to trick you. "They'll never be able to tell us apart!" they laughed as they marched right into your compositions. If you'll look at some of your papers, **they're** probably already **there**, laughing at **their** own cleverness. Little do they know that you, too, know the secret.

Princess, Miss Frag hopes that you can now use these three sound-alike words without fear. Remember this tip about good writing: When your ideas are flowing, take chances on words that you don't know how to spell. Circle or highlight them and return to them later to check for spelling. If you never take risks with words, your writing will become drop-dead boring. While Miss Frag delights in your desire to be correct, she warns that there is a difference between mastering grammar and having it master you.

Miss Myrtle Frag

58|

The Rules

Their is a possessive pronoun.

There is an adverb that indicates location (place). |59

They're is a contraction that means **they are**.

Examples:

Mr. Dietrich and his dog sit on **their** porch every evening.
    (**possessive pronoun showing ownership of** *porch*)
Dianna's gift is **there** next to the fireplace.
    (**adverb indicating location**)
Do you think **they're** going to win the game?
    (**contraction for** *they are*)

Tip: Sometimes you will see there used at the beginning of a sentence or clause, and it may seem a little confusing. There used in these ways are called **expletives**:

There are some people who always seem happy.
    (points out the **existence** of something)
I'll leave now since **there** is a visitor coming to the door.
    (still pointing out **location**, but in a different way)

60

Simple Subjects
and Predicates

Dear Miss Frag,

Oh, I could just die! Brutus is just the most popular guy in the whole school, and today he asked for my phone number, and if you don't help me I'll just die! He wants me to help him with subjects and predicates. Not because he's that crazy about learning or anything. But because he's afraid he'll have to stop playing football if he doesn't pass English. If he doesn't get to play, our team will just die because he's the one who runs the ball across that little chalk line at the end of the field.

I have a small problem. I don't understand subjects and predicates either. So I need one of your cute little stories fast!!!! Cross my heart and hope to die, I've been looking for subjects and predicates since fourth grade, and now here I am all mature and everything, and when I finally have an important reason to find them, I can't. If Brutus calls before I hear from you, I'll just die. Maybe you could send the story by email or bring it to my house. Oh, I could just die!

Clueless

62

Dear Clueless (and Miss Frag means that in every sense of the word),

Excuse Miss Frag for one moment while she takes a heaping spoonful of her anti-nausea medicine. She hopes that her devotion to teaching will override her sudden queasiness. How thrilled she is to hear that His Royal Highness of the football field is not "that crazy about learning or anything"! Miss Frag does hate to interrupt his school adventure with a learning experience.

Because Miss Frag has a heart of gold, however, she will attempt to celebrate the fact that both of you are motivated to learn, whatever the reason. Until one understands subjects and predicates, he or she cannot edit well for subject/verb agreement, pronoun case, fragments, comma splices, and run-ons. If you learn to find subjects and predicates, many other grammar rules will fall into place. Here is the story you requested:

The Owl and the Pretty Cat

The Kingdom of Grammelot was overrun with simple subjects and predicates. The problem was a tricky one indeed, for subjects and predicates formed the very foundation of all sentences. Yet huge throngs of them were using up all of the words to elaborate themselves. In fact, the entire population of sentences faced extinction. King Author called a meeting of the Knights of the Round Table of Contents. They agreed to employ experts to capture large numbers of these words for safe release.

That very afternoon, they visited Feathers and Fur, a detective partnership. There they hired Who-oot Owl (subject swooper) and Prettycat Predicate (award-winning predicate pouncer). Early that evening, the owl and the pretty cat went to see what they could find.

In no time, a carefree sentence scampered across an open field looking for some modifiers to absorb. The swooper and the pouncer, flexing their claws, began their quest.

Who-oot Owl found simple subjects by asking who or what was doing the action in the sentence. "Whooo? Who? What? What?" called the owl as he zoomed over this sentence: **Frogs croak.**

Who-oot Owl clutched **frogs** in his talons and deposited the startled word in the subject cage. Prettycat Predicate whispered, "What's going on? What's going on?" as she looked for the verb that represented the action in the sentence. She pounced on **croak** and dropped it in the predicate cage. Almost immediately, another sentence ambled by: **Twenty loud frogs had been croaking all night.**

"Hmmm, this is more challenging," Prettycat mumbled. "What's going on? What's going on?" Then with the speed that had made her a champion, she bounded on top of the verb phrase, **had been croaking**. Without delay, Who-oot Owl, called out, "Whooo? Who? What? What?" and plucked out **frogs.**

For hours they collected simple subjects and predicates. When the sentences had more than one subject and predicate, Who-oot Owl and Prettycat Predicate had to swoop and pounce several times.

As they were about to quit, Prettycat saw a huge mob of words in the distance. "Look! A whole paragraph. How will we do this?" The owl, having sharper vision, replied, "Relax, Prettycat. It's only one sentence, but it's a real doozie. We'll just have to decide what the whole sentence is talking about and ignore the other phrases and clauses. Come on!"

The air resounded with "Whooo? Who? What? What?" and "What's going on? What's going on?" as Who-oot and Prettycat charged the massive sentence: Without any thought for his own safety, and remembering the time that his mother had told him to have honor and courage in the face of danger, the boy removed his heavy boots and jumped into the community pool to rescue the little yellow kitten.

The subject swooper became dizzy from flying over so many nouns and pronouns; the predicate pouncer bounded in the wrong direction twice. At last, Who-oot lifted **boy** out, and then Prettycat immediately saw what was going on. With two pounces, she captured **removed** and **jumped**, and met her partner at the cages. The Kingdom of Grammelot was saved!

The curtain closes on this story as King Author and his knights release the captured subjects and predicates into schools around the world. It's up to you now to find them. When your teacher sends you on such a quest, listen carefully. You may be able to hear Who-oot Owl and Prettycat Predicate calling out their questions to help you.

Miss Frag urges you to ask your teacher about how to write for different audiences. Also, young lady, your mother should remind you about honesty with your classmates. Excuse Miss Frag while she nibbles on some saltine crackers to calm her uneasy stomach.

66|

Miss Myrtle Frag

The Rules

The simple subject of a sentence is always a noun or pronoun about which a statement is made. It tells who or what is acting or existing in the sentence. (You can find the simple subject by removing all of the modifiers from the complete subject.)
Questions to help you find subjects: What? Who? (What or whom are you talking about?)

The simple predicate is the part of a sentence that is the verb or verb phrase. It tells what is going on in the sentence. Often the predicate shows action, but sometimes it shows a state of being (existence, condition). (You can find the simple predicate by removing all of the objects, complements, and modifiers from the complete predicate.)
Question to help you find predicates: What's going on? (Which words tell what is going on in the sentence?)

Examples:

Frogs *croaked.*

Frogs *croaked,* and **we** *fished.*

The **bullfrogs** and **all** of their cousins *croaked*
all night.

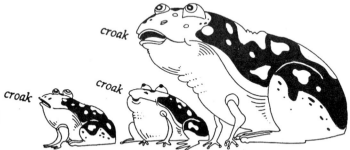

68 | The **bullfrogs** and **all** of their cousins *croaked* all night and *disturbed* the campers.

Are the **frogs** still *croaking*?

 While the frogs croaked, **the campers** *cooked* bacon.

By morning, the **frogs** *were* quiet. (Tricky! This predicate shows existing or
being instead of action.)

(**simple subject**; *simple predicate*)

169

Dear Miss Frag,

   As I always say…I'm a teacher, and the only gemstone I own is a grind-stone. Mercy, Miss Frag, I'm tired and need your help. Every year, I walk into my classroom knowing that I can transform even the most reluctant learner into a literary genius. At some point during the first reporting period, my fog lifts, and I run, screaming, out of Utopia.

   The trigger point this year occurred the day I mentioned phrases. I saw reality bound over the horizon when a student said, "Phrases? I'm an expert on those. My mom says I'm always going through some kind of teenage phrase." When the class nodded in agreement, I clung to the bookshelf for balance.

   I know the students have studied phrases since elementary school, but I don't think they care. As I teach, their eyes look like clear pools into which no stone has been dropped.

                    Utopia in my Rearview Mirror

70|

Dear Utopian,

    Good teachers everywhere frequent Utopia. Miss Frag applauds you for beginning the year with your bags packed for a long stay there. Teachers who step into the classroom with no dreams for their students should find copies of the want ads in their boxes periodically. Miss Frag is certainly not urging you to personally place the ads there unless, of course, you feel compelled to do so.

    If you want to see the students really care about phrases, show them how a well-turned phrase can brighten a paper they care about. Perhaps the power of story will give your students something concrete to grasp as the real concept of phrases begins to make sense to them:

The Crazy Phrase-ees

The people under the big tent sat in hushed silence as the ringmaster directed their attention to the high wire.

AND NOW, BOYS AND GIRLS OF ALL AGES, LOOK HIGH IN RING THREE WHERE YOU'LL SEE OUR MOST DARING ACT, THE CRAZY PHRASE-EES. EACH GROUP OF RELATED WORDS HAS TO WALK THIS WIRE TOGETHER AS ONE UNIT! YES, SEVERAL WORDS WILL WORK TOGETHER WITH A SINGLE GOAL. FURTHERMORE, LADIES AND GENTLEMEN, EACH PHRASE WILL WALK WITHOUT A BALANCING POLE. "WHY?" YOU ASK. I'LL TELL YOU WHY. UNLIKE CLAUSES, PHRASES DON'T HAVE A SUBJECT FOR ONE END OF THE POLE AND A PREDICATE FOR THE OTHER. SOME MAY HAVE ONE BUT NOT THE OTHER, SO THE IMBALANCE OF THE POLE WOULD MEAN CERTAIN DEATH! (THE AUDIENCE GASPED.)

TO FURTHER COMPLICATE THIS ACT, THE WORDS IN EACH GROUP ARE NOT EQUAL IN WEIGHT. EACH STRING OF WORDS IS USUALLY GROUPED AROUND A HEAVIER WORD. ANOTHER BALANCING PROBLEM!

IN A MOMENT, THE FIRST GROUP OF CRAZY PHRASE-EES WILL WALK FROM THE PLATFORM AT ONE SIDE OF THE RING TO THE ONE AT THE OTHER SIDE, WHERE IT WILL JOIN THE SENTENCE THAT IT COMPLETES. AND, LADIES AND GENTLEMEN, BOYS AND GIRLS, (DRUMROLL) THERE WILL BE NO NET! WITHOUT FURTHER ADO, HERE THEY ARE...THE CRAZY PHRASE-EES!

As the audience murmured in anticipation, a noun phrase eased onto the high wire. These were the performing words: **a devastating flood.**

While **flood** was not the longest word, it was the noun in the noun phrase, and therefore the weightiest member of the group. The wire sloped to where **flood** stood, and its modifiers swayed from side to side. Half way across, **a** slid into **devastating**, but by holding together, the phrase regained control. After a few nail-biting minutes, the noun phrase stepped safely onto the other platform to join the rest of its sentence:

Last year, a devastating flood destroyed the town.

As the applause thundered, the sentence slid down the pole, and a prepositional phrase bounded fearlessly onto the wire: **from the night sky.**

The phrase, led by its preposition **from**, clowned around. When **sky** wrapped its tail around the wire and executed a complete rotation, screams echoed in the tent. In a final, death-defying leap, the Crazy Phras-ee joined its sentence:

A meteorite fell **from the night sky.**

After five different teams had walked the high wire, all of the sentences stood in the ring below and bowed. The crowd, chanting "Crazy Phras-ees, Crazy Phras-ees," threw money into the circus ring. *(Some say that this is where the term coining a phrase developed.)* The phrases, worn out from their performances, stepped out to retrieve the coins and promptly fell over. Fortunately, the other sentence parts pulled them (and the money) back into line. To this day, you rarely see phrases standing alone, unless, of course, you look on the high wire during your next visit to the circus.

My dear English teacher, do not despair. Miss Frag has spent most of her life packing for and unpacking from trips to Utopia. Just about the time you're so close to burnout that your internal smoke alarm starts clanging, a class will give you an unexpected ticket back to the land where all is wonderful. Miss Frag encourages you to keep an overnight bag packed for those happy occasions.

Miss Myrtle Frag

74|

The Rules

A phrase is a group of related words that expresses a single meaning. Usually, a phrase is grouped around a noun, preposition, or verbal (gerund, participle, infinitive). A phrase may function as a noun, an adjective, or an adverb. A phrase does not have a complete subject-verb unit. It might have a *subject* or a *verb* form, but not a complete unit. When a verb is made up of more than one word, it can *be* called a verb phrase.

Phrases are often mistaken for clauses. Clauses have complete subject-verb units. They can sometimes stand alone as sentences (independent clauses), and at other times they may rely on other clauses (subordinate clauses). Phrases are their cousins, *but* do not have complete subject-verb units like clauses have.

Examples:

Some famous singers performed at the mall last night.
   (Noun phrase)
The singer **with the red guitar** is my favorite.
   (This prepositional phrase functions as an adjective telling which *singer*.)
The huge crowd gathered **at the mall**.
   (This prepositional phrase functions as an adverb telling where the crowd *gathered*.)
When we arrived, the singers **had been performing** for three hours.
   (Verb phrase)

76 | My brother, **a singer at heart**, wishes he could join the singers. (Appositive phrase)
To see this group has been my dream. (Infinitive phrase)
Singing well is a rare talent. (Gerund phrase)
Strumming his guitar, the lead singer hummed the melody. (Participial phrase)

Tips: See Miss Frag's story about clauses.
Writers may choose to use a phrase (fragment) for emphasis. When used for a purpose, phrases can stand alone. Miss Frag included such a phrase in the ringmaster's speech.

Dear Miss Frag,

Why can't teachers make up their minds? They tell us to add '_s_ or _s'_ when we want to show possession. O.K., today I used _it's_ to show possession and I thought I was going to have to call a lawyer to defend me. I never thought I would have to write to Miss Frag, but this unfairness has driven me to desperate measures. Can you help me? Please do not reveal my name or city.

Possessed with Possessives

78|

Dear Possessed,

Miss Frag would never ruin your reputation by letting your peers know that you dared to care about a grammar rule. You have asked a question that addresses one of the most common errors in writing. Nouns require *'s* or *s'* when showing ownership or relationship, but pronouns do not. *It* is a pronoun. Read this story and Miss Frag's comments at the end of her letter:

The Accidental Apostrophe

Several word friends went to Camp Wordplay. These were their names: **time, eat, to, is**, and **It** (**It** began with a capital *because* he was the group leader). One of the camp rules concerned their meals. In order to get into the chow hall for homemade alphabet soup, the words had to line up in this order: **It is time to eat**.

One day when the chow bell rang, they scurried into order...**It time to eat**. To their horror, **is** was missing! The group leader complained, "Doesn't **is** know that he's a linking verb? All he has to do is just B E here to link us together. But he's always out pretending to be an active verb! I'll have words with him when he comes back."

Suddenly, the word friends heard loud noises that began in the top of an enormous pine tree and progressed to the ground...Kaboom! Thunk! Swish, swish, crackle, snap! THUD!

They saw **is** hit the ground and watched him slowly stand. What was left of him limped toward them. He looked like this...**'s**. His beginning letter was gone, all except the dot above it. Even the dot looked strange; it was crushed into the shape of an apostrophe. Poor, wounded **is** slid into line next to **It**. Hanging on each other's words, the sentence lined up at the chow hall looking like this: **It's time to eat**.

"I hope you guys have some food in the cabin," moaned **time**, "because our injured sentence will never make it past the counselor at the door."

To their amazement, the counselor motioned for them to enter. "Nice contraction," he commented as they passed.

Some trespassers, who had heard about the camp by word of mouth, had been hanging around the campground, trying to get a free meal. When they saw the counselor let the last sentence in, they decided to copy it. They lined up like this: **Its time to eat.**

Marching up to the chow hall door, they could almost taste the free alphabet soup.

"Hold it!" shouted the counselor. "You don't make sense."

"Yes, we do!" snipped the unwelcome guests. "We look just like the group that went in before us."

"I'm afraid not," replied the counselor, and he brought the other group out to prove it. The two groups stood in lines to compare themselves: It's time to eat.
Its time to eat.

In so many words, the counselor pointed out that the apostrophe took the place of an **i**. "**It's** means exactly the same thing as **it is**," he said. "But you guys in the second group have no business on our campground. **Its** without an apostrophe shows ownership, and you don't possess a thing...especially not a bowl of Camp Wordplay's alphabet soup!"

With that, the counselor dismissed the trespassers with a warning: "Remember, you are only as good as your word." The first sentence returned to the chow hall, proudly sporting its accidental apostrophe. "Imagine that," they said. "**It's** stands for **It is**! The counselor took us at our word."

Miss Frag can explain why writers make this mistake so often. Think about possessive pronouns like theirs, hers, ours, yours, and its. If you removed the s from each one, you would still have a pronoun. That is why writers often add apostrophes as in their's and it's. Now think about another possessive pronoun, his. No one writes hi's to show possession. Why? When the s is removed, you are left with hi which is not a pronoun. Therefore, hi wouldn't make sense where you might use his. When you forget, just remember poor little 's.

82|

There are those who consider Miss Frag to be tedious. To prove that she does indeed have moments of frivolity, she has inserted a number of plays on words in her story about Camp Wordplay. Perhaps you can lighten up a bit by finding them.

Miss M. Frag

The Rules

It's is a contraction that is used for **it is**. (Make sure you put the apostrophe in the right place.) **Its** is the possessive form of **it**.

Examples:

Mom said that **it's** fine for me to spend the night. (contraction...*it is*)

The tree lost **its** leaves. (possession ...no apostrophe)

It's too hot for the dog to play in <u>its</u> yard.

Tip: Don't let the rule about nouns requiring an apostrophe to show ownership confuse you. Pronouns that show ownership do **not** have apostrophes (*my, mine, his, her, hers, our, ours, your, yours, their, theirs, its*).

References

Balanoff, P., Rorschach, B., & Oberlink, M. (1993). **The right handbook: Grammar and usage in context** (2nd ed.). Portsmouth, NH: Boynton/Cook.

Fine, E., & Josephson, J. (1998). **Nitty-gritty grammar:A not-so-serious guide to clear communication.** Berkeley, CA: Ten Speed Press.

Furnish, B. (1996). **Write right.** Bloomington, IN: Phi Delta Kappa.

Hacker, D. (1991). **A Writer's Reference** (3rd ed.). Boston: Bedford Books.

Tarshis, B. (1992). **Grammar for smart people.** New York: Pocket Books.

Wadden, M. (1990). **Easy reference grammar guide.** Logan, IA: The Perfection Form Company.

Weaver, C. (1996). **Teaching grammar in context.** Portsmouth, NH: Heinemann.